Christmas 1989

Betty,

Thanks for all you
have done for me over
the past months. You
are a special person.
"A friend loves at all
times" Proverbs 17:17

Love
Chris

Making His Heart Glad

Making His Heart Glad

Marie Chapian

BETHANY HOUSE PUBLISHERS
MINNEAPOLIS, MINNESOTA 55438
A Division of Bethany Fellowship, Inc.

Copyright © 1989
Marie Chapian
All Rights Reserved

Published by Bethany House Publishers
A Division of Bethany Fellowship, Inc.
6820 Auto Club Road, Minneapolis, Minnesota 55438

Printed in the United States of America

Library of Congress Cataloging-in-Publication Data

Chapian, Marrie.
    Making His heart glad / Marie Chapian
        p.   cm.

    1. Meditations.   I. Title.
BV4832.2.C5226   1989
242—dc20   89-37343
ISBN 1-55661-083-1   CIP

Dedicated to
Dorothy Jordan,
My Mom and Friend

MARIE CHAPIAN, Ph.D., is well-known around the world as an inspiring author and speaker. She has written over twenty-four books with translations in thirteen languages. She has received many awards for her writing, including the *Cornerstone* Book of the Year and the Evangelical Christian Publishers Association Gold Medallion Award.

A Heart for God Devotionals

His Thoughts Toward Me
His Gifts to Me
Making His Heart Glad

Contents

Introduction

This is the third book in the *A Heart for God* devotional series. In the first two books God speaks to us in personalized scriptural form, and now in *Making His Heart Glad* the believer's voice is also heard. In the form of prayers or open letters to God, these conversations are meant to reflect the voices of those who long to know God, to understand His thoughts and will, and to find their perfect place in Him.

An intimate walk with God includes facing the questions, doubt and fears—even terrors— that only He can bear for us and respond to so tenderly. We dare not make light of our weaknesses or sorrows, for God does not gloss over pain and suffering. He embraces these just as Christ caressed the leper.

Making His Heart Glad speaks to us of the reality that our human needs and outbursts are precious to the heart of the Father. In our quest for well-being and pursuits of love and belongingness, God is very much present and involved.

These daily readings are to be read slowly and meditatively. The Lord will speak to your heart as you prayerfully enter His presence. The scripture verses at the end of each reading are offered to stimulate further reflection.

These conversations between the believer and God represent us all, and so it is my prayer that you will hear your voice in here, too—that a chord deep within you will be touched by the Holy Spirit. May you be moved gently and soundly toward the warm embrace of God, the place where He leads us—where we make His heart glad.

One With You

Lord, I want your Word alive in me,
so much so that I am no longer
ruled by the cares
that surround me.
I want your Word to sink into my spirit.
I want to be filled with you
and all that you give of yourself
to your children.
I want to be dominated by your personality.
I want your thoughts to permeate mine.
I hunger for you
and for your peace
that passes my meager understanding.
I know you reward those
who diligently seek after you,
and I earnestly seek, long, ache
to know and be one
with you.

Hebrews 11:6

Seize and hold fast
the faith and hope you cherish and possess.
I, who have promised, am reliable
and faithful to My Word.
I will be faithful to you.
The secret of the sweet, satisfying
companionship of the Lord
is yours.
If you live by the Holy Spirit,
walk also by the Spirit; and
when you call upon Me,
I will hear and answer you.
To be one with Me,
to walk one single path,
is to fulfill your calling
and the highest aspiration
of a human being.

Hebrews 10:23; Galatians 5:25; Jeremiah 29:13;
Psalm 25:14

Success

Lord, teach me about success.
Show me through your Word
the skills of achieving success and excellence
in this life.
You've said that you're able
to furnish us with all grace,
favor and earthly blessing
so that we are always and in all circumstances
furnished in abundance;
so I ask you for godliness
to accompany the talents you have given me.
Give me reasoning skills
and godly thoughts
because if I have these I will always act wisely.
Give me enthusiasm for life
and godly energy
because if I have these I have the keys to
satisfaction.
You are all things to me, Lord;
My happiness
doesn't come from what I achieve,

for you have shown me
that excellence and success
are achieved in you.

What you have asked for is good:
    I know your heart.
I give you My thoughts regarding many things.
    I created your mind
in order that you might be filled with Me,
    possessing wisdom and intelligence.
I created your hands
    to accomplish the works I have called you to—
hands of honor and integrity.
    I gave you eyes
that you might see with the insight of God,
    and ears to hear
with the sensitive Spirit of God.
    I created your voice
for my pleasure.
    As you lift it up in My name
all heaven rejoices with you.
    And sometimes I am more glorified
when you are silent.
    I am glorified in My people.
I have called My people to glorify Me.
    I give My people a purpose.
It is to live as I have lived and

do as I do.
Because you ask
 be prepared to receive.
Freely I give to you.

2 Corinthians 9:8

A Heart of Kindness

Lord Jesus, help me
to be more kind.
I find it easy to be kind
to strangers,
to disembodied, telephone voices—
people who live at the edges
of my attention.
But when it comes to loved ones,
family,
people of enduring importance,
I am brutish,
indifferent.
The times when I'm kind remind me
that I'm not kind at all.
I am like a sounding brass.

You cannot be truly kind without My kindness
  pervading your soul.
Kindness is a sister of love,
  planted deep in your spirit
by My Spirit.
  It develops and grows as love does.
Anger and frustration
  dry the roots of kindness,
wither the buds of love.
  Yet,
one small act of kindness can
  reopen your soul
to the heart of heaven.
  (Even a sip of water brings
a prophet's reward.)
  And dear one,
you are responsible
  for knowing this.

Ephesians 4:32; Galatians 5:22–23, 25;
Matthew 10:41, 42

Do I Have to Be Responsible?

I don't *like* to take responsibility
for my behavior, Lord.
I want to blame
mistakes and faults
on other people,
or on the way I was brought up,
or on any excuse I can think of . . .
If I behave poorly, it's because
the checkbook's too empty,
or someone was rotten to me,
or the kids were hard to handle,
or the car broke down—again.
It's people—or circumstances.
Right?
It's never *my* fault
that I'm the way I am—
is it?

You can never grow a garden
    if you continually trample on the seedlings.
You may "accept yourself as you are,"
    but soon the weeds
will twine around your neck
    and you will have to cut off your conscience
to go on.
    Others may seem to accept
your poor behavior,
    but thorns and stubble
mar your life
    where respect might have grown.
The full harvest of love
    demands respect;
tolerance is not love;
    fear is not love;
resignation is not love.
    When you wound another's heart,
that wound is
    twice yours.

Proverbs 3:3; Romans 8:7; Galatians 6:2, 10;
Matthew 7:16, 20

I Hate to Feel Guilty

Feeling guilty . . .
I'll avoid it at all cost!
I don't *like* to admit I'm wrong.
Besides, feeling guilty
lowers my sense of self-esteem
and I feel horrible.
Who needs it?

You try to heal your own wounds
    by avoiding and denying
that you are flesh—
    weak
and perishable.
    You make excuses for your humanity;
you lie to yourself
    in hopes that you may be a god,
not needing to change,
    beyond question or reproach.

But your own image,
     which you wish to reflect,
is dim,
     smudged.
And when heaven looks at you,
     you rarely look back
because you are not free
     from guilt.
To come to inner peace,
     you must forsake your image
for Mine,
     because I created you
to bear My likeness.
     Don't resist Me, little one;
your guilt and shame were crucified
     on the cross with My Son.
So you need not deny guilt
     any longer—
simply release it.
     This is true freedom,
true forgiveness.
     In the freedom of My love,
you find
     your true self.

Isaiah 64:6; 1 Peter 2:24; John 3:17; John 12:25;
1 John 1:9

My Behavior Hurts

Lord, I hurt the feelings
of a loved one today.
I spoke unkindly.
I accused.
I ranted.
I was *selfish*.
It's not the first time.
Why am I abusive?
Why do I hurt the ones I love?

You have accepted a blighted lifestyle
*   as okay.*
You believe that arguments, rudeness, fights
*   and displays of temper are okay.*
You have thought you could hurt, insult,
*   sulk and manipulate others without consequences.*
You have falsely believed your ungodly behavior
*   is justified.*

Do you think those who live in peace and harmony
    are other than human, without feelings or
    problems?
I have commanded you to be kind,
    to love one another
because it is entirely possible for you.
    Come, climb into My heart.
Let the kindness you will find in Me
    overtake you
and restore your likeness to Me.

    I AM perfect love and kindness,
and I dwell in your spirit.

    The inner life of your spirit, made alive
by My Spirit,
    is full of light and ability.
All you need is within you.

    Link your mind to My mind.
Allow yourself to accept your life as Mine.

    I am not frustrated, worried or bitter.
Contrary to your suspicions,
    which are not too entangled to root out,
you are safe in Me.

    You are not upon the earth to
do it damage
    but to ease its travail,
and you can do it.

Romans 12:10; 1 Corinthians 13:4;
Ephesians 4:32; Colossians 3:12; Romans 8:22;
2 Peter 1:5–7

Lost and Found

I've gone
far from love.
The air is stifling
and unclean here.
Choking.
I slipped away so quietly,
unnoticed by most.
At first my words began
to mimic the darkness,
and I drank the wine
of vanity and pride.
I stopped reading the Word.
And then I stopped hearing from you.
I became defensive,
competitive, full of my self:

> And now the jokes
> aren't all that funny.
> The darkness is a prickly coat.
> My body has strange aches.

Paranoia salutes me daily.
The laughter is grating.
I have caring friends,
but I am uncomforted.
My soul is starved,
and though I live I am dead.
I never talk about you.
I am like Peter in the Bible:
Nobody knows I know you.

———————◇———————

My child,
let Me restore and heal your heart.
Let Me gather your sorrows and sins
and restore wisdom and life to you.
You have eaten of
the world's agonies.
Now, come and dine
where your name is cherished
and where your God
will satisfy your hunger
with good things
for My eye is ever upon you.
Will you allow yourself
to be loved again?
I will blot out and forget
every transgression;
I will revive your starving soul

and restore you to myself.
Come home.
You will taste what you hungered for
    in Me.
No lifestyle,
    or social "circle,"
Not even your goals
    will feed you.
Seek, and you will find
    Me.
Come home.

Isaiah 43:25; Isaiah 57:17–18;
Jeremiah 29:11, 13

Clean

O Lord, how can I cleanse my ways?

Look for yourself in My Word.
   Are your ways reflected there?

Psalm 51; 1 John 1:1–9

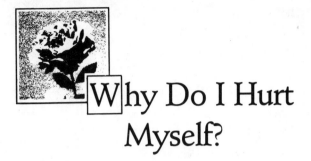

Why Do I Hurt Myself?

Why don't I trust
being *happy*?
It's as if
a brightly colored
candy cart,
decorated in gold
and filled with delightful gifts
and things to eat,
parked right on my doorstep
with its music playing cheerfully
but I keep throwing rocks at it.
Sometimes I think if pain were handed out
in bundles,
I'd be the first in line.
Of course, I'd complain bitterly about it,
because I don't stop to question
why I make choices that hurt myself.
I simply writhe on, not knowing

what a brightly colored candy cart
is all about.

———————————

I see you
  cringe and fumble
at the brink of blessing.
  The prospect of a happy heart
frightens you.
  At the moment of contentment,
you crumple and withdraw.
  You are unaccustomed to thinking
in terms of true delight and joy.
  You dream of being happy;
you have fantasies and
  you use words like "seeking fulfillment"
and "making this life count,"
  but you don't allow yourself
to understand what those words mean.
  You pray, but don't allow Me to answer.
You seek Me, but by a wrong name.

My thoughts toward you are for good,
  and not for evil.
Whatever is born of Me
  is victorious over the world
and its death-dealing ways.
  Strengthen your faith in Me,

and My joy in you
   will increase.
I give you all grace,
   every favor and earthly blessing
in abundance
   because I have created you
to bear My gifts.
   You are Mine.
You are my precious treasure.

Isaiah 50:2, 3; 2 Timothy 1:7; Jeremiah 29:11;
1 John 5:4; 2 Corinthians 9:8; Isaiah 43:1

I Don't Like Myself

Lord,
why couldn't I have been born
different?
I don't think I can change.
I've never been ambitious,
or particularly motivated
to anything big or great.
I dream big,
but I guess I just can't make it.
Maybe I'm one of those
vessels of clay
the Bible talks about.
But I'm so unhappy.
Misery follows me.
I hate my life.

Behold, you are beautiful, My love.
I call you out of lethargy

and the stupor of lies and misinformation
  you believe about your life.
Rise up,
  leave self-condemnation behind you;
Come. Take My hand
  and I will show you
a heavenly mirror
  so you can see your true self
as I see you.
  The winter of your misery is past,
and spring, new-green and sweet,
  is here to warm your soul.
Love Me,
  and you will love yourself.

Song of Songs 1:15; Song of Songs 2:10–13;
1 John 4:16, 19

To Please Him

Lord,
if only I knew that *you* were pleased with me,
I wouldn't be prey
to fear or doubt;
I wouldn't grind my teeth
with worry.
If only I knew that *you* were pleased with me,
I would have peace—
contentment beyond my dreams.
The fear of death
wouldn't tap at my door each night.
The fear of loss and pain
would no longer wrack my dreams.
I wouldn't feel fragmented,
rushing
from
place
to
place
seeking
approval

and
love.

Lord,
how can I please you?

———◇———

I have shown great mercy to you;
I ask you now to offer your life
    as a living sacrifice to Me.
Choose—now—
    to present your body, soul and mind
to Me.
    What I ask is your reasonable, rational
and intelligent service:
    holy, devoted, consecrated
in respect and love for Me.
    This pleases Me.

Romans 12:1, 2

Help With Finances

Lord,
I work hard,
but still there isn't enough money.
I love you and love to serve you,
but my checkbook
is depressing.

Carefully study
the words I have given you.
Absorb My command:
"Love the Lord your God
and serve Him
with all your mind and heart
and with all your entire being."
Then you will have plenty,
for you will know My ways.
I am your Shepherd;
you will have no want.

Is your burden too great to bear?
Be wise
    and let My holy management take charge
so that My blessings
    overtake your lack.
Give, and you will be given much;
    it will be poured into your hands—
more than you can hold.

    The way you give to others
is the way I will give to you.

Deuteronomy 11:13–15; Psalm 23;
Deuteronomy 28:2–8; Luke 6:38

The Sword of
the Spirit

Dear Lord,
when I face the demands
and pressures of the day
and I rush
to conquer, persevere and overcome,
I need your standard
of excellence.
I need your principles
and attitudes to guide
and assure me,
because I tend to surge ahead
like a soldier running blindly
into battle.
I run, charged like lightning,
my sword raised,
weapons clanging at my side.
I slash wildly
and actually manage a few kills—
but your way in battle

is to go *before*,
not after.
Am I swinging my sword in the dark?

———————

*Pressures, demands and hardships
are not your enemies;
    they are facts of life.
You can, as you say,
    "persevere, overcome and conquer"
because I have told you in My Word
    you can.
But the appropriate sword
    at all times
is wisdom.
    A wise person seeks light for the path.
But a foolish person
    is like a wild boar crashing about
in the dark.
    Recognize your enemies
and use your sword wisely.*

Ephesians 6:17; Ecclesiastes 2:13, 14

Lord, Remove the Trials

Lord, if there were no
suffering on the earth . . .
it would be so wonderful.
Can't you just work some special miracles
and eliminate all life's trials?

You are mistaken to think
   the absence of trials
will bring happiness.
   You gain insight into My ways and purposes
by careful study of My Word.
   I show you the ways of
skillful and godly wisdom.
   It is not wisdom
to wish for a magical cure
   for the sufferings of life.
Rather, pray
   for deliverance from sin,

for strength and reinforcement
    in your inner person
by the mighty power of My Holy Spirit.
    Become rooted in love,
founded securely on love,
    and suffering will not threaten you so.
Come to know and experience for yourself
    the rich goodness of My love,
which surpasses every false
    peace that the world offers.
Then you will be filled with
    My fullness—
wholly filled and flooded with Me
    and the sting of suffering
will be removed.

Ephesians 3:16, 17, 19

Surrounded

Lord, all around me
is turmoil,
unhappiness and discord.
It's rubbing off
on me.
Help.

— ◇ —

Dear one,
  be careful!
Don't conform
  to the disenchantment of the world
nor allow its customs, fears and habits
  to influence your behavior.
Allow My love and power
  to transform you daily
and raise within you
  the strength of dignity.
I will renew your mind constantly
  and keep you pure.
I am within you

to give you
  supernatural energy and enthusiasm.
Separate yourself.
  This is how you prove for yourself
what My good and acceptable
  and perfect will is.
Surround yourself in Me.
  for I am loving you,
  cherishing you,
  always.

Jeremiah 31:3; Romans 12:2; 2 Corinthians 6:17

Close to God

Lord,
how do I know you more?
How can I know your closeness?

Only as you know Me
    can you become like Me.
Close to Me,
    you won't want to leave
the most beautiful "place"
    a human being can experience—
the interior of My heart.
    I understand the pull of the world
on your attention and energy,
    its influence upon your thinking.
That is why you must keep your ears open
    to My voice.
When the sounds of the world
    drown out My gentle urging,
you feel alone
    and separated from Me

where you have no
     real self
or place to stand.
     But when you are so close to Me,
living in the blazing center
     of My heart,
My heart is glad,
     for that is when
     we are one.

1 John 2:15–17; 1 John 3:1–3

An Independent Spirit

Lord, I don't understand
how I can be independent *and* dependent
at the same time.
Alone, I'm strong (I thought).
Dependent, I'm weak (I thought).
Am I not supposed to stand
on my own two feet
and make decisions
on my own?

———◇———

*Dependent upon others for what I have given you
already*
    is foolishness.
You have the illumination,
    the light, strength, courage and wisdom
of My Spirit.

But to be one with My Spirit
is to divinely depend on Me.

I will be what I promise to be—
do as I promise to do.

John 14:15–31; Matthew 6:19–24

Easily
Influenced

Not only am I influenced by ungodly people,
I'm equally influenced by the godly.
Whatever the current trend is in church,
I go along with it.
"Go with the flow"
is a life-pattern for me.
I talk like everybody else does.
Dress like they do.
Am I hearing you, Lord, or am I following
the Christian, "acceptable" path?
I never make waves—anywhere.
I just go along quietly
earning acceptance.

My heart is filled with compassion.

*Your ache for approval gives you
non-identity.*

You are not yourself, but someone else—

Who?
    But when I see you I see My beloved,
the one I formed in My own image,
    unlike anyone else
in all heaven and earth.
    When you dare to lose acceptance,
you are free to
become yourself
    and please Me.
Dare to make waves.

Matthew 9:36; John 15:15

Feeling Weak and Ineffectual

I don't know
if I can stand up
for myself.
I don't feel strong
or capable,
and I don't think I really
touch
anybody else's life for you.
This makes me feel bad
because I know I should
have an effect
on my world.

My dear child,
*   you are the salt of the earth.*
You have only begun

to taste my savor.
Because you are Mine, you are also the light
that gives My light to the world.
A city that is built on a hill
cannot be hidden.
And people don't hide a light under
a bowl.
They put the light on a lampstand.
Then the light shines for all people
to see.
You have only begun
to shine.
Eat of the salt of My Word;
look to My brightness.
Then you will live
so that others will praise your Father
in heaven.

Matthew 5:13–16

Feeling That I'm Not "Enough"

Lord, life is so short.
I am a stranger
on earth, a passerby,
a temporary resident.
I feel insignificant,
unnecessary.
Others are more talented,
more intelligent,
more attractive.
I am dismayed
at how bland I am.

Your feelings of inadequacy
    are not of Me.
They come from hungry,
    Wordless

mind-wanderings.

Your first desire must be for Me
and for My Word.

Feed upon My teachings;
meditate, ponder and study My words to you.

Blessings and worth
will rise like living water
up through your roots,
like a tree firmly planted by rivers
of water.
Then there will be no fear of cold, heat
or drought;
you can rest in confidence.

I am your river.
Gain My wisdom
and you will love your own life.
Nothing in My hand is small.

Psalm 119:11; Psalm 103:4, 14, 15, 17; Psalm 1:1–3;
Jeremiah 17:7–8; Isaiah 58:11; Proverbs 19:8

A Faithful Friend

You've always been a friend to me, Lord,
even though I've not always been a friend to
you.
You've always been faithful to me,
but I haven't been faithful to you.
You've always given me your best,
but I've given you so little.

———◇———

Your Lord is merciful and gracious,
  slow to anger,
and overflowing in mercy
  and lovingkindness.

Psalm 103:8

# On My Own

Alone,
uncherished, single,
on my own.
Lord, I'm not sure I can endure.
I try, I brave it out,
I have not fallen
yet;
but it makes my heart heavy
to mean so little to anyone else
but you.
People rush past me like shadows;
the guard dogs of past hurts
are intimidating but
I am so in love with living
I am breathless,
sleepless.
You alone know me.
And that's because I trust you
and because your love never changes,
wears out, nor ends.

Alone or not alone
it's good to be loved by you.

I am the Lord your God
   and I hold your right hand;
I say to you, fear not, I will help you.
   I lift you up.
I rejoice in you.
   I love the righteous.
I bless you with an upright heart
   and put you in right standing with Me.
I take pleasure in you;
   My delight and joy,
I am your lover and friend.
   Will you take the glory and beauty
I give to you
   and be glad we are one?
Do not be afraid of loneliness:
   I heal the brokenhearted;
I cure your pains and sorrows.
   I open My hand and satisfy you
with favor.
   I fulfill the desire
of everyone who loves Me;
   sadness shall not overwhelm you.
For I rescue you
   from behind the high walls you built

to protect a shattered heart.
I tell you this so that
*   My delight may remain in you,*
a fountain of joy and gladness
*   full*
and overflowing:
*   I will not*
leave you alone.

Isaiah 41:13; Psalm 146:8, 9; Psalm 149:4;
Psalm 147:3; Psalm 149:5; John 15:11

I n Sickness

Lord, please heal my body.
I plead day and night for health,
but yet I am sick.
I cling to you
for strength and understanding:
Where are your healing wings?
At times my hope grows weak.
My heart becomes faint
and I am exhausted.
I grope for your hand
to lead me to health.
But it's not there.
Lord, please don't forget me!
Restore my strength.
I've trusted you
and I will continue to trust you.
I stand confident in your mercy
and lovingkindness.
I will sing to you even in sickness,
because you have dealt fairly with me.

Dearest one, in whom I am well pleased.
    I will never forget you.
Can a mother forget the child
    she is nursing?
In Me is your help and sustenance.
    A picture of you is indelibly
imprinted on the palms of My hands,
    and your concerns are ever before Me.
I know your physical limitations,
    but I am also intimately involved
with your emotional and spiritual life.
    Look to your soul.
Both body and soul
    were bought with the blood
of My Son Jesus.
    Because He died for you
and paid the price for your sins
    and sicknesses,
your body is the sanctuary
    and the holy house of My Spirit.
My Spirit does not need
    a body that is robust and full of health
before making it His home.
    I enter when I see the sign
of a heart filled with God.
    Your body doesn't bless the world

as your willing spirit does.

My child, drink in My words;
read and study them and keep them
in the center of your heart,
for when you are united to Me,
you are one in spirit with Me.

Our union transcends bodily sickness
and health.

My words are life to you, healing
and health to you,
but remember above all,
the springs of life flow from your heart.

Yes, I heal. I deliver. I restore.
Practice excellence
in the caretaking of your body—
yet know the prized
and holy condition
is spiritual wholeness.

Psalm 13:5, 6; Isaiah 49:15–16;
1 Corinthians 6:19–20; 6:17;
Proverbs 4:20–23; Jeremiah 30:17a

Family Problems

Lord, I can't get along with my family.
Our lives are miles apart at times.
I'm not at all patient with them.
Sometimes I just want to run away,
go where there is peace and understanding.
Is it too much to ask for—a harmonious home?
Maybe I could find happiness somewhere else.

If you turn to Me,
    listen to My instruction
and correction
    through My Word,
you will discover the way of life.
    Your loved ones need to see Me in you.
There is too much of you in the way.
    I want to release you
from the chains of discontent,
    bitterness and anger

that fill the rooms of your mind.
    I know your inner longing for respect.
Can you give to those you love
    what you most need yourself?
Can you become kind to one another—
    tenderhearted, compassionate
and understanding,
    forgiving one another
just as I have forgiven you?
    Godly relationships are formed
of My Spirit,
    and by selfless work on your part.
I will help you.

Proverbs 10:17; Proverbs 11:29;
Ephesians 4:31,32

The Good Samaritan

Lord, when I read the story
of the good Samaritan,
I realize
I'm not a very good testimony of your love.
In fact, I don't think I represent you well
at all.
I don't help people
if it means going out of my way,
or if it doesn't pay off,
and I'm only nice to those who "count."
I wouldn't give a second glance
to a destitute figure lying in the dust.
I just pray it'll never be me.
I want to be a blessing,
to bear fruit for you,
but I'm afraid I'm a failure
in that department.

No branch on the vine
    can produce fruit alone.
Growing in Me,
    building your character in Me,
becoming like Me
    is the fruit of intimacy
with Me.

    I am the Vine and you are the branch.
If you remain in Me and I remain in you,
    you will produce much more fruit
than the one deed
    of the good Samaritan.
But without Me you can do nothing.

    Don't be as the branch that is broken
off the vine and thrown away.

    You are not helpless,
you are unformed.

    Remain in Me
and follow My teachings;
    then you have the privilege
of asking whatever you will
    and I will answer.

It is My desire
    that you draw nearer to Me;
in your special secret place in Me
    there is no task

too offensive for you.

I have called you to do many works
that you do not know of yet,

and in your human strength
they would seem impossible.

But because you love Me,
nothing will be impossible
to you.

Luke 10:30–37; John 15:1–7; Luke 1:37

First Things in
the Morning

In the morning,
    My compassion greets you.
The morning stars sing together,
    exulting in the new day, and the angels rejoice.
I am the Morning Star:
    I shine on you with life, newness,
beauty and strength.
    Lift up your eyes and see
that new mercies await you
    as you rise to meet the day.
Embrace what is yours:
    I give you all you require
to feed the needs
    of every hour;
I enlighten and invigorate you;
    I fill your eyes, ears and every nerve
with acute awareness—
    Light and Life are Mine.
The work I have called you to

is My work,
this day, My day.
Arise!
Your light has come.
The Morning Star is
risen in your heart,
and there is a whole world
waiting for you to discover.
Seize the opportunities
that are before you this day.

Revelation 22:16; Lamentations 3:23, 24;
2 Peter 1:19

The Troubled Heart

I'm falling apart;
my life is in shambles.
No more can I lie
or pretend things are fine when they
aren't.
Nothing is going right,
and just when I think I'm making some
headway,
the bottom falls
out
again.
I can't take this stress and anxiety.
I'm riddled with fear; I don't sleep at night.
I rip up the night with my complaints
and I don't even know how to
pray.
God, where are you?

Why have you lost sight
    of My goodness?
You complain and murmur—
    but don't you know I want
    to rescue your soul
from the battle within you?
    I will face your enemies;
they contend with Me.
    But you torment yourself.
    Stop.
    Quiet your soul.
    Cast your burdens upon Me:
the onslaught is too much for you.
    I know your frame,
physically and emotionally.
    I know how you are hounded
    by pressures
that are Mine to bear,
    not yours.
You constantly seek a person
    to help you and save you from your troubles.
But I tell you to turn to Me first.
    I am your strength
and the reason
    for your life.

You may not know how to pray
*   but talk to Me, read My Word;*
study to know Me.
*   I will be known by you.*
You would love Me if you knew Me.
*   You would relax*
and shake off the
*   wolves of despair*
that grip your throat.
*   Give Me your concerns.*

Psalm 55:18, 22; 1 Peter 5:7; Psalm 118:8, 9;
Isaiah 12:2

The Sound of Singing

I wish I had a better voice.
I try to sing, but . . .
my ear is like stone.
I wish I could sing
like others.
Lord, could you please bless me
with a good voice
and some musical talent?

———◆———

But I love to hear you sing
*   right now.*
I love your praises
*   and your sounds of joy.*
I am your song,
*   and when you sing*
the whole creation hums
*   in harmony.*
The voice is the instrument

to stir human souls
but it is the heart
that reaches the ear of God.
There is music in great sounds
of joy and jubilation!
There is music in the crashing waters,
in the sound of wind in the trees.
But there is no music as delightful
to My ear as the sound of My children:
because it is your heart that I hear.

It makes My heart glad
to hear you
because your sounds are pure and true.
My Holy Spirit springs
from your spirit
in the form of music,
and the sounds you make
are holy.

They refresh and renew your soul;
they bless My heart.

Sing to Me a new song.
Even in diversity,
sing to Me.
Even in trial
and what you think is your darkest hour,
sing to Me.

Sing to Me, for I am your Beloved;

sing to Me a tender, loving song.
*   I am your song.*

Psalm 118:14–16; Psalm 33:1–3; Psalm 144:9;
Isaiah 5:1

The Radiant Life

Lord, I feel so dull.
Like my life is without gloss or sparkle.
I'm easily bored,
and when I'm with others
I'm quiet and shy.
I don't have much to talk about
and I'm afraid people must find me
bland and uninteresting.
Help me, Lord.
When I study the Bible,
I see the Holy Spirit is not shy and listless.
The Spirit of God is powerful and mighty.
What's wrong with me?
Can you change me?

I want to polish you
with wisdom.
When I give wisdom,

you gain strength and confidence.
Wisdom makes your face to shine,
    to glow and radiate.
Wisdom helps remove
    a shy, self-indulgent countenance.
When you set your heart on Me
    (not on yourself),
when you reject fear and shyness
    and recognize them as enemies
of your calling in Me,
    when you put the sin of indifference
out of your life,
    then you can lift up your face
to Me in confidence.

    Then you will feel steadfast and secure,
and you will fear no more.

    You shall forget your misery.
Those who are wise
    radiate My beauty,
and they turn many to righteousness.

    They give forth light like the stars
and shine forever in My kingdom.

    My precious one, in wisdom
look at Me now,
    and be transfigured
into My very image

in ever-increasing glory.
Allow My reflection to shine
    through you.

Daniel 12:3; 2 Corinthians 3:17–18

Things That Last

Lord, I've worked hard
and long
to provide home, food, clothing—
the basic needs of living.
In fact, most of my life has been spent
providing for daily needs.
My most pressing concerns
have been bills,
purchases and income—
and usually it's more
out-go than in-come.
When I'm not working to pay
for what I've bought,
I'm out buying more
or repairing and maintaining
what I already have.
(This is supposed to be the good life?)
I look around me and wonder
where all this will be in a hundred years.

Will my epitaph read:
"A soul who really knew how to shop"?
I want your best, but I wonder
if I've found it?

I have called you
to represent Me in the workplace,
not merely to make money
for your needs.
I have called you
to reflect the heart and personality of your Lord.
This is the essence of life.
If you spend your time toiling
for things that only perish,
what have you left?
Strive to produce, instead,
the lasting fruit of righteousness,
which endures into eternal life.
I have laid the foundation for you
to build your life upon: My Son, Jesus.
If you build upon Him,
whether preaching,
practicing medicine, or law
or washing windows,
your work is My work.
Do all that you do unto Me
and do what you do with all your

best effort.
Works are tested by the fire
of holiness and integrity.
Examine your heart.
Do you work with faith, hope and love?
And does everything you do
demonstrate the greatest of these?

Ecclesiastes 9:10; 1 Corinthians 3:10–14;
1 Corinthians 13:13

I Want to Be Your Disciple

Lord, I've been a believer for a long time and I think
I lead a good, clean life.
It's important to me to walk upright
and to do good to others,
because I want to please you.
When I read in your Word
about being a disciple,
I think I already
am.
But lately . . .
there's a gnawing in my soul
and I'm not content with myself as I
should be.
I really want more of the Truth,
and I want to be your *disciple*.

Who is My disciple?
    Who is the one who brings pleasure
to the Holy One?
    If you live in Me, closely united with Me,
no gaps between us—
holding fast to My teachings,
and taking joy in them
then you are truly My disciple
    and My pride.
You will then know the Truth.
It will be in your bone and fiber,
in your breath and tissue.
    This is the Truth
that sets you free
    and makes you My disciple.

John 8:31–32

Why Do Some People Seem More Blessed Than Others?

I can't seem to overcome
the trials of my life.
And yet I look around me
and see other people
leading happy, good lives
and I wonder why I can't
be more like them.
I can't understand why
I have to suffer so much,
and why most other people
don't have
to go through
as much as I.

Quiet your anxious soul, My beloved,
    and feel the gentle breath
of God.
    Be still and experience
the sweetness of heaven.
    Rest.
    Listen.
Those who are led by the Spirit
    are Mine.
This Spirit births in you
    the words of sweet contentment:
"Abba," you say,
    and I answer, "Yes, child, I am here."
My beloved, you inherit all I have;
    in My Son, you share suffering
as well as glory.
    Pressure, affliction and hardship produce
endurance;
    and endurance produces
faith, integrity and maturity of character
    (do you want to stay a baby?),
and these produce
    the habit of joy.
Your troubles need not possess you
    and your heart need not
be desolate and dark with envy.

Let My Spirit teach you
to triumph in your troubles
and enjoy the glory of God.
The Holy Spirit raised My Son, Jesus,
from the dead,
and this same Spirit dwells in you,
restoring your mortal, short-lived, perishable
self
in Me
continually.

Romans 5:3, 4; Romans 8:5b, 9; Romans 8:14–17;
Romans 8:11

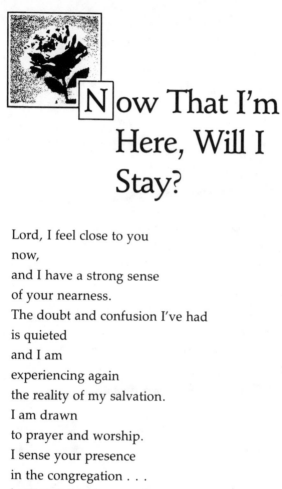

Now That I'm Here, Will I Stay?

Lord, I feel close to you
now,
and I have a strong sense
of your nearness.
The doubt and confusion I've had
is quieted
and I am
experiencing again
the reality of my salvation.
I am drawn
to prayer and worship.
I sense your presence
in the congregation . . .
but Lord, I feel unsteady.
Will it last?
I don't wholly trust
what's happening to me.

I have drawn you
  out of the control of darkness
and have transferred you
  into the kingdom of My Son,
who is Love.

  This is not an emotional experience;
it is a spiritual reality.

  (You are not accustomed
to unemotional decisions.)

  The blood of My Son was poured out
from His body on the cross of Calvary
  and has bought you forgiveness,
cleansing and renewal.

  I will always liberally supply your needs
in all areas of your life,
  including your needs for self-control
and sound, clear thinking.

  You've made poor choices before.
Your mind has been veiled
  and your feelings ruled you.
Because of the riches in glory
  in Christ Jesus,
be encouraged, be strengthened,
  be confident:

I am the source
of all you need or want,
and I will not let you fall.

Colossians 1:13, 14; Philippians 4:19

The Uncontrolled Mind

I daydream my life away.
The life I lead in my imagination
is far better than the one
I lead in reality.
I didn't think there was anything wrong
with that.
I'm not a bad person.
I don't get into trouble
and I'm a Christian.
But sometimes
I daydream about ugly things;
I imagine horrible events and
I scare myself.
People talk to me and I tune out.
Things go on around me that I'm not even
aware of.
My mind wanders when I try to read

or concentrate,
and the only thing that captures
my attention
is the television set.
Help me, Lord, I'm out of control.

———————◇———————

When you came to Me, My child,
  I opened the gates of heaven to you.
You shucked the leathery shell
  of your old sinful nature
in exchange for a new nature in Me.
  By My Spirit
your new nature can be sharp
  and clear-sighted
because My perfect love casts out
  old lifeless habits.
My Spirit doesn't meander aimlessly
  without a certain purpose for you.
That is why you can take charge
  of your thoughts.
Take them captive. Be disciplined.
  Escape the empty pit
where dreaming goes
  sour like old milk
and mind-wandering turns
  crude and evil,
and you become discontent with

your life.
Set your mind on things above.

    Why do you live as if you still
belong to the world?

    Set your mind on things above.
And keep it there
and love will keep you.

Colossians 2:13; Colossians 2:20; Colossians 3:2;
Proverbs 13:4

Getting Upset Over Little Things

Lord, I let things bother me
and I get so upset
that I become physically ill.
Even little things bother me.
I explode inside.
My stomach churns.
I see injustices
everywhere.
Nothing seems to go right.
I try to keep above things
and not get upset
when things go wrong,
or people upset me,
but I can't
help myself.
Inside I am always hurt
or outraged.

You are wearied-out,
  exhausted,
through judging and criticizing.
  You need steadfast confidence
in My justice.
  The external thoughts and devices
of the mind atrophy,
  but the life of the Spirit of God
within you is renewed day after day.
  Striving causes you to forget
that "the just shall live by faith,"
  and you become anxious, flustered,
and your thoughts are scattered
  like soot.
Where are your thoughts?
  If they were stayed on Me,
peace would caress each path
  of your mind.
In place of turmoil,
  My peace would rule in your heart.
My peace is not only an option,
  it is your holy calling.
Let not your heart
  be troubled.
Stop watching and counting
  the sins and cares of the world.

Affix your heart to Mine
    and learn of My Majesty.
In the beauty of a heart
    filled with Me
there is peace.

Hebrews 10:36; 2 Corinthians 4:16;
Hebrews 10:38; Isaiah 26:3;
Colossians 3:15; John 14:27b

Eyes to See

Lord, I want to see
    as you do;
    I want to look at life
    through your eyes
    and perceive the world,
    people and situations
    from your perspective.

To understand My Word requires an awakened spirit,
    a soul made alive by My Spirit.
Then when you read and meditate
    upon My words,
they have the meaning I intended for you,
    and you become one with My Word.
So much of your life is concerned
    with what your eyes see
and not that which makes the eye see.
    Look at the life-center
of your work, your ministry, your play.
    Can you see to the very center?

It is the place that is at once tiny
    and enormous, where the still small voice
of God resides and yet is large enough
    to contain the world.
The place of seeing doesn't lurch ahead
    like an untrained dog on a leash.
Wait upon the Spirit of God
    to reveal wisdom.
Do not be indebted to the world,
    which you are called to bless.
Let your eyes be the handwriting of your soul.
    When you see the world as I see it,
it will respond to the love in your
        eyes—
    a window upon the heart of God.

John 10:10; John 10:34–38

A Waste of Time

Lord, I don't feel I do
enough
for you.
I want to accomplish more,
but my good intentions aren't enough.
I'm ashamed of myself.
What can I do?

My Beloved,
*   Why are you so hard on yourself?*
With whom do you compare
*   yourself?*
Don't think that serving Me
*   means only works.*
The happy heart is like a medicine
*   and it pleases Me more*
than you know.
*   The discontent, irritable heart*

is like a thorn in your spirit
    and a sorrow to Me.
I do not put demands and pressures
    on you; I have given you a free will
to keep or offer to Me.
    In the very freedom of owning your will,
you take more on yourself
    than you need.
I am here, waiting
    to be Lord of your time.
Live as though
    mercy and kindness
were written
    in the manuscript of your heart.
This is the way to make your life
    spiritually prosperous
and to use your time
    fruitfully.
Blessed are the merciful
    for they always show mercy
in My kingdom.

Proverbs 17:22; Titus 3:5–7;
Proverbs 3:3; Matthew 5:7

Storms in the Night

I dread nights like this.
Listening to the thunder
and watching the angry black sky
split open by lightning
reminds me of stories I've heard
of people being struck down dead
and whole towns being destroyed—
destruction and death and
an infuriated God above.
This fear of storms
is like my fear
of every kind of invisible enemy,
not to mention God.
I've always wondered, *Lord,*
what horrible sins were committed by people
who are struck dead by "acts of God"?
I ask myself, why should I be spared?

My dearest,
    I watch over you.
There is no danger you can face
    in life
that I cannot handle.
    There is no enemy too big
for Me.
    Be not afraid.
You have made a place for Me
    to live in your heart,
and where I am
    there is perfect serenity.
But you have created
    so large a place in your mind
for fear to thrive.
    How big is the home you've built
for your faith?
    Where are its
pillars, buttresses and beams?
    Where are its beautiful furnishings
and treasures of art?
    Faith is beautiful, gleaming,
mightier than a fortress,
    and it requires much space—
in your heart and mind.
    Faith cannot be pinched

by the fingers of fear.

My servants shut the mouths of lions,
stop great fires,
and are protected from evil weapons.
They are weak, yet are made strong.
And so are you.
Build a shelter of faith in you,
where we two may dwell.

1 John 4:18; Hebrews 11:34; Proverbs 12:21;
Isaiah 50:10

Finding Favor

I'm always trying to please
someone,
and I'm seldom successful.
No matter how hard I try,
I can't always be sure
of finding favor.
Most important to me
is that I find favor with you, Lord.
Show me how I can win
your stamp of approval.
Help me to be satisfied
finding favor with you.

Look at My Son, Jesus.
   He pleased very few people,
yet He was perfect love made human.
   He was sinless, loving and good.
He pleased Me in every way
   and was obedient to the point
of death on the cross:

105

He is your example, your high priest,
your Teacher and your Savior.

So you need not earn my favor:
it is My free gift to you
called grace.
If you have My favor,
why do you strive so hard
for human approval?

Am I not able to give you favor among others
as I will?

When your ways please the Lord,
I make even your enemies
to be at peace with you.
So be at peace;
rest from your fruitless labors
to earn love and acceptance.

You only exhaust yourself.
People who are
of the world
and not of Me
crave the approval of men
but are never satisfied.
You are not of this world.
You are My child.
I show you what is good
and what is required of you:
justice, love of mercy

and walking humbly with Me.
These show you love Me
with your entire being
and make My heart glad.

Matthew 3:17; John 8:29; John 12:45;
1 John 2:15–17; Micah 6:8;
Deuteronomy 10:12, 13

Regrets

I was so wrong to do what I did.
If only I'd known then
how sorry I'd be at this moment.
Now there's no way to get back
what I've lost.
I was blind and selfish,
and even though I want to make amends
it's too late.
I'll never get back what I've lost
because of my sin. . . .
Oh, Lord, I'm filled with regret
and remorse.
Please, please . . .
help me and forgive me.

I am a forgiving God.
    Turn to Me with your whole heart
and you will find Me;
    love Me with all your heart,
soul and mind

and you will not trip into sin.
Trust Me with your whole heart,
    not leaning on your own limited
understanding,
    and you are on the safe path.
Your life is ever before Me:
    Do not worry about the former things
or berate yourself for the past;
    watch, for I will do something new—
I will spring forth as a surprise to you.
    I am He who makes a roadway
in the wilderness
    and rivers of clear-flowing water
in the wastelands of your life.
    I will not remember your sins.
My lovingkindness will hold you up.
    In the midst of your
multiplying anxious thoughts,
    I am there to comfort you.
My consolations can delight your soul.
    Let Me be your strength
and your life.

Joel 2:12; Matthew 22:37; Proverbs 3:5;
Isaiah 43:18, 19, 25; Psalm 94:18, 19

Being Afraid

Lord, sometimes I'm overtaken with fear.
My skin grows cold,
my breath comes hard,
and I feel utterly helpless.
I'm afraid of so many things—
of certain people, of being alone,
of death, pain,
not having enough money. . . .
Lord, the list never ends.
Please,
I just can't help myself.

———

Do you not know that
    in Me you are
safe?
    When you live in My shelter
you are in a stable place;
    you are in the shadow of the Almighty
whose power no enemy can withstand.
    I am your refuge and your fortress,

your God on whom you can rely.
Lean on and trust Me;
I will deliver you
from all traps and snares.
I will cover you with the holy feathers
of My protecting wings.
There is no reason for you to be afraid
of night terrors,
nor of any evil plots or slanders.
In the place of safety
you will not be afraid
of any nuisance
roaming the earth.
You will not be afraid
of any destruction,
real or imagined,
that attempts to darken the noon.
Though you may observe the world
stumbling and falling around you,
you will walk in your integrity,
which is your faith,
and you will be unscathed.
Make a home for your heart
in the secret place of the Most High,
the place where you were born
to live.

Psalm 91:1–7

In Need of Discipline

Lord, I don't like correction.
I don't like being told what to do,
and I don't like saying no to myself.
I just want to live my life
the way I want to.
I know it's not pleasing to you
to be self-willed,
and I *do* want to change.
But it's painful to begin the process.
Denying myself makes me feel
like a child again
without any control over my life.
Rules and discipline make me feel
as if I'm being unfairly punished
by a world bigger than me,
and I just want to live my life
with a mind and will of my own.

For the time being,
　　no discipline seems joyful to you.
You may find it grievous and painful,
　　but let Me assure you, dear one,
discipline benefits you in every way.

　　Through discipline's work
there is an enormous harvest
　　of beautiful living:
The fruit is love,
　　joy, peace,
patience, kindness,
　　goodness,
self-control;
　　and you are drawn
into oneness with Me
　　where there is no agony.
Through discipline
　　your thoughts and actions are charged
with life's energy,
　　and you are free to be your real self
in all your integrity and strength.

　　The unbridled life
without discipline
　　produces weakness and an impoverished spirit.
Therefore, take charge of your thoughts and drives.
　　You are called to show strength of character

and to face challenges without flinching.
  In time, you will love My discipline
and the blessed fruits it brings.

Hebrews 12:11, 6; Galatians 5:22;
2 Corinthians 10:5; Ezra 10:4

The Full Armor of God

Lord, I want to do as your Word instructs;
to put on the full armor of God
and stand against the plans and wiles of the
devil.
I know I must stop blaming my troubles
on people and situations,
because you tell us
we don't wrestle with flesh and blood.
The war is between the believer
and principalities, powers, rulers
of darkness and spiritual wickedness
in high places.
It's all so overwhelming. . . .
I'm tired of being defeated and upset
by every devilish prank.
Teach me to be a strong warrior,
wise and armed for you.

My complete armor empowers you
to resist evil and perform mighty deeds.
You have My Truth
around the center of your being;
you have My integrity and morality
at the gates of your heart.
You have peace and stability
as your foundation.
Everywhere your foot treads
you bring the gospel of peace.
You are covered in faith,
which is like a shield,
so the flaming missiles from hell
cannot bombard you.
Wear your salvation as a helmet,
and carry as your fiercest weapon
My Holy Word,
which is your sword.
These weapons make you
a soldier of the
cross,
skilled in warfare,
empowered by union with Me.

Ephesians 6:10–18

Overcoming Tiredness

Lord, I'm making a choice
to overcome
lethargy,
and I'm determined to do it
your way—through your Word.
I don't want to be a tired, worn-out person
barely able to get through the day.
I want to build myself up
emotionally and physically
by carefully searching your Word
for instruction and help.
Lord, I need your help now.

———◇———

And so you have My help, dear one.
I will speak;
you will listen
and be strengthened.
My words to you

are as apples of gold.
They are life;
    they are Me.
Why should your soul sink down
    in heaviness?
I raise you up and renew your strength
    as I promised from the beginning.
Lift up your hands that hang down
    and rejoice!
Your vigor greets you.
    I have said
the weak shall proclaim strength
    and so you shall.

Daniel 11:19; Proverbs 25:11; John 1:1–4;
Psalm 119:28; Hebrews 12:2; Joel 3:10b

The Perfectionist

Lord, I always thought
doing things perfectly
was the only acceptable way.
I work hard at everything I do
and I expect others to do the same.
It's important
that I do everything to the very best
of my ability.
Isn't that what you ask?
I like to be first, I like to win,
I like a job well done,
I like orderliness and neatness,
I'm just a perfectionist.
But I'm never truly happy,
because things are never as perfect
as I want them to be.
Please help me make things better.
Help me improve.
Help me be more perfect.

Oh, dear one! I don't ask you to be Me,
    only to be like Me.
If you are like Me,
    you are gentle, kind, patient;
you are tenderhearted, honest,
    and your motives are pure.
If you are like Me,
    you are not driven by vain and crushing demands
for excellence
    (I don't crush you to make you better).
Are you afraid you are not acceptable
    unless you achieve more
and are better than others?
    Is your drive for perfection
to prove yourself
    to yourself?
Search your heart, beloved.
    Your stressful ways
have hurt others.
    Your thoughts and words have been
judgmental, harsh
    vindictive.
When you are driven with
    ungodly perfectionist drives,
you cannot hear the soft, tender voice
    of My Spirit calling you,

guiding you,
loving you.
I have told you
My goodness will satisfy you.
I satisfy the longing soul.
For what does your soul long?
I do not promise you perfection;
I promise you grace.

Romans 8:29; 1 John 4:16; Luke 10:40–41;
Psalm 107:9; 2 Corinthians 9:8

In Search of Silence

Life has become so loud, Lord.
It is a thundering clamor
and I feel I'm tossed
in the outer darkness
of a raging storm.
I hunger for silence.
So I run to a place
to be alone
in the quiet—
but the storm is there, too.
Loud, disjointed,
interrupting the stillness.
I realize the storm is *me*.
I rage, I rush, I tear up the days
and the nights
with my anxious thoughts
and I have made my bed in noise.
I hunger for the sound
of silence.

To become silent
     before Me
is to release control
     over your own life
and destiny.
     Your true life
is in the silent interior
     of your heart
where you have not
     yet traveled.
You have stayed outside
     to watch the parade,
to dance with the clowns,
     to wear their glittering costumes,
and to ride the plumed pony.
     You sing the songs
of cheated lovers
     and you are cheated.
The world of your senses
guides you.
     Yes, I am in the mountains and the oceans,
birds and beasts,
     flowers and fruits,
deserts and plains—
     all of which I created
with a word.

But your soul is the home
of My Spirit.

Listen there for My quiet voice.
Journey toward love,
leaving your noisy plans and dreams.
Be still in the fiery gaze of My love,
even as Moses
stood before the burning bush.

Resist the impulsiveness of your senses,
your intellect,
your emotions,
and come to the secret, inner home
in your heart
where My Spirit lives.

There I speak to you lovingly
and in silence.

Ezekiel 3:27; John 1:3; Genesis 2:7; 2:2;
Psalm 46:10; Acts 17:28; Exodus 3:2–5

Prayer of the Desperate

Lord,
I feel the world closing in on me.
I'm surrounded
by disaster and trial.
I can't take it.
Please hear me and help me.
Don't let me be swallowed
by the problems that threaten me daily.
I'm at the end of my rope—
desperate.

I hear you, dearest.
   I am your refuge and strength.
   I am always near you
   and available to help.
Do not fear.
   Even if the earth should change
and the mountains slip into

the belly of the sea—
and even if the oceans roar
    and foam,
and the hills quake,
    I hear your voice
calling out to Me.
    I will rescue you.
I will go out
    to battle for you.
I will not allow you to be utterly
    shaken.
Trust Me.
    Though you walk through the pit
of gloom and death,
    do not be afraid,
because I am at your side.
    Let My goodness and mercy
embrace you.
    Take My hand and
let Me comfort you.
    You are Mine, My child
Give Me thanks
    even when you don't feel like it.
Recount My marvelous works
    and wonderful deeds.
All is not swallowed
    in evil.
Be glad and exult in Me.

Sing praises—
I am on the throne
and you are safe.

Psalm 46:1–3; Psalm 55:16–18a, 22; Psalm 23:4, 6;
Psalm 9:1–2, 4

Favor With God

Lord, I want to live my whole life
as a gift to you,
presenting every day
my body and all my faculties
as a living gift.
I want to be a joy
and a source of pleasure
to you.
This is my reasonable
and intelligent gift.
It is the only way
I want to live.
Keep me from the temptation
to become beguiled
by the world's external
pursuits and promises.
I want my mind
to be renewed continually,
and transformed

by your ideals and attitudes.
It fills me with awe
that I can prove
your good and acceptable
and perfect will.
Oh, Lord, to know your will!
To know what pleases you!
This is my heart's longing
and sole desire.

———◇———

My beloved is Mine,
    and I am My beloved's.
The wise inherit glory and honor,
    and I delight when you choose
that which is wise.
    You will know My will
and find favor in My sight
    as you continually forbid
selfishness, hypocrisy, and hatred
    from rooting in your mind.
Write My words of love
    on the tablet of your heart
and be clothed with a new, spiritual self
    (which My Spirit
    constantly renews,
    forming you more and more
    into My likeness).

You are My chosen representative,
    precious and much beloved
by Me.
    I love your gentle ways
and tireless patience,
    because these give you
power to endure whatever comes
    with a calm and steady
disposition.
    Wrap yourself in the tapestry
of My love,
    which binds all things together
in perfect harmony
    and keeps you in the center
of My eye,
    and I shall call you
My beloved
    and My friend.

Romans 12:1, 2; Song of Songs 2:16;
Proverbs 3:25a, 3–4; Hebrews 13:16;
Colossians 3:10–12, 14; Song of Songs 5:16b

Choices

Dear Lord,
I need your help at this time.
There are many decisions
before me
—so many—
and I don't want confusion
to overpower me;
I don't want to become nervous,
impetuous, or unsure of myself.
Give me confidence to know
I can make the right decisions
because you are within me
and will not allow me
to fall.

Whatever you do,
whether in word or in action,
do everything in the name
of My Son, Jesus,
and in complete dependence

upon Him.
Allow My words
    to have their home in your heart
and thoughts
    and allow the Holy Spirit
to sift the questions that arise
    through the pores of divine reason.
You will not be confounded,
    for I am here to instruct you
and show you the way you should go.
    I am guiding you with My holy eye.
Listen with your spiritual ear:
    My whisper is soft,
coming from the depths
    of you—you'll hear it
like a voice behind you,
    "This is the way, walk in it."
I guide you when you turn to the right
    and when you turn to the left.
Be quiet and have confidence.
    I am your strength
and decision-maker.

Colossians 3:15, 17, 23; Isaiah 50:7; Psalm 32:8;
Isaiah 30:21, 15

God As the Employer

My job has become more of a workout
than work, Lord.
I have thrown myself into this job
so I can get ahead
and have security
because I'm in a competitive field
and I must perform well
if I'm going to be a success—
or even to survive.
But even so, I must still do
all that I do
as if *you* are my employer.
I realize that I am your servant
and your friend in all things,
not only in my religious life
but on the job, too.
I want my hard work
to be for you.
I want it to transcend

joylessness and exhaustion.
Teach me, Lord.
Teach me, Holy Spirit,
guide me.

———◇———

It is thrilling
*   to do all that you do*
heartily
*   with your soul,*
for it proves a happy heart.
*   When you do*
all that you do
*   for Me,*
and not for recognition,
*   monetary gain,*
or approval of people,
*   you release yourself*
to take joy in something more rewarding
than merely surviving:
*   I speak of your inheritance*
as a servant in My kingdom
*   where there is no competition.*
My rewards are endless,
*   and you can experience them daily.*

Begin with a happy heart.

Your work is of great value to Me.

Colossians 3:23; Romans 12:11; Joshua 24:15;
Psalm 1:1–3; Proverbs 17:22

Ears to Hear

Dear Lord,
I don't know why
I can't seem to be
victorious
over despondency.
I spend a lot of time
alone,
just thinking.
And the more I think, the worse I feel.
People tell me
I'm a nice, quiet person;
but if they knew
what I was thinking,
they wouldn't say
I was so nice.
I long for relief.

I have told you to abstain
    from all appearance of evil—
and that includes

the taste, smell, touch
and sound of evil.
    Your thoughts are
crashing cymbals,
    disrupting the voice of love
and the sound of peace.
    Let your thoughts
listen for and hold on to
    that which is good.
My Spirit will give you
    spiritual ears
to listen to the thoughts
    as they enter your mind.
Ask each thought as it proceeds
    to your heart,
"Are you of the Lord?"
    Repel the intrusive
and senseless thoughts
    that destroy your soul's health
and joy.
    Rise up like a warrior
against self-destructive lies
    that have seduced you in the past.
You have chosen to embrace
    many hurtful thoughts.
But the world's ways of thinking
    are not yours, little one.
Fill your mind with thoughts

gleaned from My Word;
attune your ears and fix your mind on
thoughts worthy of reverence,
honorable thoughts that are
just, pure, lovely, kind and gracious.
Your entire being
will sigh a holy sigh
and praise Me
for a mind renewed
and for ears to hear
the Truth.
Come soar with Me.

1 Thessalonians 5:21–22; 1 Corinthians 2:15a;
Philippians 3:8; Matthew 9:4; 1 John 5:4;
Philippians 4:8

How Do I Pray?

Help me, Lord,
to unite with your will
so I may pray wisely.
I can't see ahead into the future.
I may pray to be saved from things
that may be for my good,
or I may pray for those things
that would ultimately mean harm.
I can't, in my finite mind,
grasp your infinite plan.
My wants and desires are strong,
and they can crowd out
your gentle urgings and warnings.
There are many concerns on my heart
and I don't know
how to pray about them.
I'm not sure what your best is.

My dearest one, My Holy Spirit
    comes to you
and bears you up in your weakness.
    He knows that you do not know how to pray,
and so He meets your spirit
    in a holy union
and pleads on your behalf
    the passions and yearnings
of your heart
    with unspeakable depth
and power.
    I search your heart, My beloved,
and I know what is there.
    I am one with the Spirit:
My mind and intentions
    are in perfect alliance with the Spirit,
and He intercedes and pleads
    on your behalf
in accordance with My will.
    You can be assured
I hear and answer,
    for we are partners
in bringing about
    My will.
All things are working together,
    fitting into My plan

for those who love Me
and live in My design and purpose.
Pray,
keeping within the fathomless walls
of My Spirit.
Pray on all occasions,
for all needs and requests,
being alert with spiritual ears
and always ready to pray
for the family of God.

Romans 8:26–28; Ephesians 6:18

What Is Normal?

Lord, I don't know
what is *normal* anymore.
I feel torn
between my "religious" life
and the world around me.
It seems crazy to me
to be so alone in my feelings
when the world looks at me
as if I'm weird and strange.
I don't do what my old friends
are still doing,
and they think I'm abnormal.
My friends at church
tell me it's normal
to be abnormal.
Am I weird and strange?
   What *is* normal?

I am all that is normal.

I am sanity.

I am life.

There is a false and sinful nature
that you once tried to build up
and develop
without Me.

You tried to blend with the darkness.
Your real life began at the moment
of surrender,
and your abandonment
of the false world.

Your false nature slowly dies
to make room for the growth
of your real self in Me.

It can seem to you
that My ways are strange
and unnatural,
but that is only when
you have accepted the false world
as real and good.

Do not become so accustomed
to an insane,

unnatural way of life
that you question Truth.
Do not be afraid of divine sanity.

Deuteronomy 11:26–28; Romans 8:2;
1 Peter 4:2–4

Forgiving When It's Difficult

Lord, I want to be forgiving—
but it's hard.
I feel hurt and angry
and it seems hypocritical
to simply mouth the words
I'm *supposed* to feel.
In my heart there is not
one drop of forgiveness.
There is pain and sorrow
and oceans of anger.
I've been hurt and wronged.
I want to scream in protest;
I want to fight
and get back what I've lost.
How can I forgive
and ask your blessing

on those who have hurt me.
I need a special touch
from you.

———◇———

Dear one, your Lord and Savior
    hears and sees
and understands.
    I have compassion.
I am not heartless and
    demanding,
and I do not ask you
    to deny your emotions,
nor do I ask you to mask
    your hurts from Me.
It is important to Me to
    expose your wounds to My love,
healing and soothing
    in My refreshing balm.
Let Me caress
    the heart that aches.
Release your sorrows to Me.
    Let Me take them
on My own body,
    which I gave for your sake
when I went to the cross.
    I, too, was treated badly.
I was beaten, whipped, spit upon.

Nails were struck through my flesh;
I was left hanging—
    innocent of every sin—
to die.
    Give Me the pain you feel
and I will save you
    from its lasting sting.
I forgive you of every wrong
    and you have the power
to forgive, also.
    So release yourself
into My rest
    and pray that
the wicked will forsake their way
    and unrighteous persons their thoughts.
Be glad and rejoice in My mercy.
    I know your adversities
and I am here to love
    and to ease the struggle.

Colossians 3:13; Mark 11:25; Hebrews 9:14;
John 16:15; Hebrews 2:17; 1 Peter 2:21–22;
Isaiah 55:7; Psalm 31:7

The Battle Against Sin

Father, help me to resist sin.
Give me the power
to turn away from temptation
and to stand for what I know is
right, true and good.
I want to be strong.
I want to be clean.
I want to be pure before you.
It's a battle
and sometimes I don't know if I'm winning.
Only you can help me.

———————

Take heart, dear one.
 Fleshly drives
cry out loudly—
 but your soul will not
be satisfied with sin.
 You will not

feel truly at peace
or at home
with worldly substitutes for
sublime joy in Me.
I am woven into the texture
of your being
and you are woven into Me:
Sin is at war with your real nature,
the nature of God in you.
Sin is unnatural,
out of harmony with yourself
and with Me.
I give you power
to overcome.
For greater is the throbbing
presence and power
of God within you
than all of Satan's temptations.
Lock My words in your heart,
where they will protect you.

Luke 17:21; Romans 8:9–11; 1 John 4:4;
Romans 6:2; Psalm 119:11

A Wife's Prayer

Help me to love my husband, Lord,
to cherish him
the way he deserves
to be cherished.
I want our love
and friendship to grow
as we develop
an ever-deeper bond
of mutual respect
and caring.
We promised faithfulness,
for better or for worse,
through difficult times
and good times.
I pray that through the hard times
we keep our sense of humor,
that we become strengthened,
more resilient.
And when the good times
come,
help us to praise you—

for every good and perfect
gift comes from you.
I want to be a good wife,
a strong, wise, capable woman
my husband can be proud of.
Bless his work, his heart, his life
with joy and fulfillment.
Help me to make his life
easier, sweeter and happier,
because I love him
with a love that is complete.
I don't expect him to fulfill
my life: I leave that up to you.
I don't demand he be something
he can't be: I let the Holy Spirit work.
I thank you, Lord, for this man
you have given to me to love
and to honor.
To share the joys
of life with.
It is easy to do
with you at the center
of our marriage.

A wise and intelligent wife is
    a gift from Me,
and your husband has found

that which is
true and good.
    You are more precious
than jewels;
    your value exceeds that
of rubies or pearls.
    I have called a woman to be earnest
and strong in character,
    virtuous, wise and capable.
When she marries
    she is a crowning joy to her husband.
It is with great delight
    that a man can trust and rely on his wife
with confidence.
    She will comfort, encourage
and do him good
    all the days of her life.
Your husband is your friend
    and your lover,
and I will guide and help him
    to love and bless you
and to treat you
    as I treat you—
for I love you
    with a perfect love.
I give you My special blessing
    and ability to love your husband
as you love Me,

for he is worthy of your love.
In your union
  of harmony and mutual respect,
as joint-heirs and partners
  in the kingdom of God,
I am glorified.

Proverbs 19:14; 31:10; 12:4; 31:11–12;
1 Corinthians 7:3; Ephesians 5:2, 24

A Husband's Prayer

Father, thank you for my wife.
Help me to be the kind of husband
you want me to be
and to love my wife
as you love her.
She is like part
of my own body,
precious and near.
She holds me up,
blesses me and respects me.
Help me to show her how much
I respect and cherish her.
Keep me from being
overbearing and inconsiderate
and expecting her
to be an extension of me
and my concerns.
Remind me to allow her
to be her own person.

You did not create her to be
my servant
but your pleasure.
Bless her, Lord,
for she is my delight
and my friend.

———◇———

The calling of a husband
* is a high calling.*
As Christ is the husband
* of all believers*
(in the Church, the Bride of Christ),
* so you are the husband*
of the woman
* I have given you.*
Love her,
* honor her*
and listen to her.
* Nurture your friendship,*
for she will be
* a foundation of strength for you*
and a faithful voice of encouragement.
* Your marriage will be*
unshaken by the storms
* of life.*
Love her as you love yourself,
* let her grow and bloom*

as I lead her,
    and never quench My Spirit
in her.

    Together you are a mighty team,
a joy to heaven
    and a delight to Me.

Proverbs 18:22; Ephesians 5:25, 28; Psalm 149:4;
1 Corinthians 7:3; Proverbs 5:18–19; Luke 12:32

Thank You, Lord

How can I thank you
for your mighty hand of love
on my life?
How can I thank you
for giving me back my health,
my strength,
my youth?
You have added to me
every blessing,
every delight—
and all because
I learned the secrets
of receiving joy
from *within*!
I learned that the wellspring
of your life
is within me—
no matter the circumstances.
Oh, Lord,

you heal the brokenhearted
(which I was),
and you bind up the wounds
of the crushed
(which I was).
You have soothed my pains
and sorrows,
and I am once again
clear-eyed and laughing.
My joy is restored;
you have lifted me up.
Great is the Lord!
Your understanding is
inexhaustible and boundless.
Because of your great love
and tender mercy,
I am happy and blessed;
my soul prospers
and I shall never again
look for light in darkness,
nor search among the dead for life.
Forever will I thank you.

———————◆———————

I take pleasure
    in My children
who worship with
    hearts of thanksgiving.

It is a good thing you choose
    when you allow My Spirit
to emanate through every fiber
    of your being.
All things change
    and become new to you.
I spread My hands out
    to you,
to show you great
    and wonderful things.
I am gracious and merciful
    in all My works,
and I am always near
    when you call
upon Me.
    I will fulfill every desire
because I rescue, preserve
    and bless
all those who love Me.
    My dear one,
I have much more
to give you.

Psalm 147:3, 5, 6; Matthew 22:32; Luke 24:5;
Jeremiah 30:17; Psalm 147:11; Psalm 144:15, 18–20;
Psalm 145:16

Prayer of the Single Person

I am glad that I found you
in time
to be glad and rejoice
in my life,
instead of storming heaven
daily
for a mate
as so many other
single people do.
I'm glad
that I have found immense
satisfaction
in being loved by you,
and sublime delight
in providing a dwelling place
for your Spirit.
My tears are less frequent,
and my laughter is light,
without strain

or caution.
I have stopped hunting,
and come to a place of rest.
You have laid your hand
upon me
and given me a true and
complete contentment.
Thank you, Father,
for hearing my prayer,
for having mercy upon me
so I don't waste my days
in tortured pleading
for the mate—
who may never come.
Thank you for the peace
I now have in trusting
your perfect, lovely timing.
And at the times
when I feel alone
and unloved,
help me to remember
your love for me
and the unique
opportunity I have
to spend myself
in serving you.

Single doesn't mean
   unloved.
It doesn't mean
   half a person,
half a dream,
   half a life.
It means your Lover
   and your Spouse
is your God.
   I love you as
My betrothed.
   I have called you
to myself.
   And where can you go
from My Spirit?
   Where can you run
from My loving presence?
   I am within you;
I am everywhere.
   Let Me love you.
I know you better
   than you know yourself.
I know your needs
   and your wants.
I know what you love
   and what pleases you.

I formed you in your mother's womb.
   My eye has ever been
upon you.
   It is good to trust Me,
for I will never disappoint you.
   Allow My Spirit to express himself
through you more and more.
   Be open and giving,
for the world hungers for living examples
   of My caring heart.
You are My delight
   and My friend.

Psalm 146:9; Psalm 139:7–18; Luke 6:38

The Secrets of Prayer

Lord, are there secrets of prayer
that I need to know?
I want to climb
into the depths of you
and learn the power of prayer,
so that I am meeting you
fully, totally
in lovely communion.
Enrich my prayer life
with your Spirit's
guidance
so that I may be pleasing
to you in all things.

◇

When you pray:
    Come to Me
with the knowledge
    that you are standing
before Me

in complete oneness
with Me.

Let your cleansing
be complete
and your mind be clear
of obstacles.

This is a holy experience,
and it will expand
to include
your entire being.

You are not merely reciting prayers,
nor are you saying empty words.

When you are intimately
sensitive
to My closeness,
your soul is awakened.

This divinely appointed
state of being
does not remove you from
this world
so you can make your home
in the clouds—
no, rather your entire being
is made alive
and aware
of the world around you.

You see its beauties
as never before.

You see My face
in the affection
of your loved ones,
and you long to give
even more to them
to make their lives richer, better. . . .
Prayer is not
just a thing you do,
because My Spirit prays
within you constantly.
The inner eye of the Spirit
reveals My presence
in all things.
I created you to share
in My being.
You are loved by Me,
and in loving Me back
you are what you were
made to be.
I am the Vine
and you are My branch.
In prayer you breathe
in My breath,
you are alive with My life,
and there is no prayer
that will go unanswered.

Isaiah 65:24; Matthew 21:22; Hebrews 4:16;
Jeremiah 33:3; 1 Thessalonians 5:17; John 14:23

A Leader's Prayer

My one desire in life, Lord,
is to serve you
with all my heart.
I want to please you
in all I do.
Give me your wisdom
to know the difference
between your good and your best.
I am dedicated to serving you
faithfully and completely
with every waking hour.
I want my life to praise you
and tell the world
of your wonderful love.
I want to win souls
for you and to help those
in need.
Rather than looking
to fill my needs,

I want to look
to where I am needed.

———————

My servants are as bright
    shining stars in the heavens,
for they turn many lost souls
    to the Light of Life.
Your obedience is your strength,
    and you shall save many
from death.
    You are a servant of all people;
you are to love your enemies and do good,
    lend when you have nothing to lend,
and hope for nothing in return.
    Your reward is in Me.
Stretch out your hands
    to the poor and the needy,
be ready to speak a word to the weary,
    and bind up the wounds
of the downtrodden.
    Be strong, steadfast,
unmovable,
    for I am with you.
Stay alert, watching
    with a steady eye.
You are always My ambassador.
    Accept and suffer

every hardship;
    do the work of an evangelist;
perform the duties
    of your ministry
without grumbling.
    Remember, beloved,
I deliberately choose
    what the world would consider
weak and foolish
    to put the wise to shame.
But you are My anointed minister.
    I am with you
always.

Proverbs 11:30; James 5:20; Luke 6:35;
Proverbs 31:20; 1 Corinthians 15:58;
2 Timothy 4:5; 1 Corinthians 1:27

Why Did I Say That?

Lord, it seems I'm always
saying the wrong thing
and misrepresenting myself.
Sometimes I think
people get the wrong impression
of me.
They don't look beyond externals
to the heart.
I know you see my heart
and you love me,
but, Lord, I want
to be a good example
and to represent you well.
So please help me
to guard my mouth.

*Honor and integrity
    are to be highly valued.*

A person of honor
       has made the effort
to store up good things
       in his or her heart.
That which fills
       your heart
is what proceeds
       from your mouth.
Keep and guard your heart
       with all diligence, dear one,
for out of it
       flow the springs of life.

Luke 6:45; Proverbs 4:23

Blessedness

Lord, I like to imagine what
it would have been like
to live in Jesus' day—
to be His student and disciple.
I like to imagine
sitting at His feet on the grass
as He sat teaching,
or walking alongside Him on the road
as He shared with His closest friends.
I imagine eating meals with Him,
sitting by the sea of Galilee in the setting sun,
listening to Him teach from a little boat.
But, Father, I can hear Him now.
I can hear Him through the Scriptures.
The Holy Spirit makes every word
live and breathe
and come alive in me.
I can hear the divine heartbeat
of heaven and earth;
I'm alert to the blessedness
prepared for the children of God.

The blessedness of My children
*   is a joy so perfect*
nothing can come near it.
*   Human happiness is dependent upon*
what the world gives.
*   Your blessedness*
cannot be taken from you.
*   I bless My precious ones*
who are poor in spirit,
*   who realize their utter helplessness*
and who trust Me wholly.
*   Theirs is the kingdom of heaven.*
I bless those who mourn,
who sorrow and despair
for the suffering of the world;
*   I comfort them.*
I bless My meek, long-suffering,
patient children;
*   they shall inherit the earth.*
I bless those who hunger
for more of Me.
*   They shall be satisfied*
*   completely.*
I bless those who are merciful
and hold the hand
of those who hurt;

I shall give them mercy.
I bless the pure of heart,
those whose mind and motives are pure;
  they shall see Me.
I bless those who are peacemakers,
who look for another's highest good;
  they are My sons and daughters.
I bless those who suffer for Me,
whose crime is faith in Christ;
  theirs is the kingdom of heaven.
I bless those who are persecuted
and slandered for the sake of My Son;
  their reward in heaven is great.
Hear and learn
  the heart of your heavenly Father,
which your Savior taught
  and which He continues to teach . . .

John 16:12; Matthew 5:3–12

Prayer for Greatness

Lord, help me to:
come forth like Lazarus
sing in prison like Paul
pray with wisdom like Solomon
dance like David
love like Ruth
be faithful like Daniel
be courageous like David
be valiant like Deborah
be worthy of praise like the
    Proverbs 31 woman
and have the patience of Job.

If you would have the greatness
    of a hero—
would you also have the suffering?
    The greatest is the least,
and true greatness becomes

the lowly servant.
As for you,
you will walk
in your integrity,
and in you
I will be well pleased.
You will bless
the name of the Lord,
the Author and Finisher
of your faith.

Matthew 18:1–4; Matthew 23:11; Psalms 11–12;
Revelation 21:6, 7